ELECTROCULTURE

BY

JUSTIN CHRISTOFLEAU

In the same collection:

– *Electroculture, the Application of Electricity to Seeds in Vegetable Growing*, by Alexander Carr Bennett (1921)

– *French Patents in Electroculture* (to be released in November 2016)

Disclaimer
Despite all our efforts, we could not find information on Justin Christofleau's heirs. They are free to contact us about this new edition.

Talma Studios
60, rue Alexandre-Dumas
75011 Paris – France
www.talmastudios.com
contact@talmastudios.com

Cover image: © Jdazuelos | Dreamstime.com

ISBN: 979-10-96132-08-9
EAN: 9791096132089

ELECTROCULTURE

BY

JUSTIN CHRISTOFLEAU

Member of

The Society of Scientists and Inventors
of
France

ALEX. TROUCHET & SON
1a Padbury's Buildings, Forest Place
Perth, Western Australia

1925

JUSTIN CHRISTOFLEAU
Knight of Merit of Agriculture. Gold Medallist of
Society of Encouragement for National Industries.
Member of Society of Scientists and Inventors of
France. Foundation Member of National Society
of Agriculture. Member of Association
of Manufacturers and Inventors of France.

MR. J. CHRISTOFLEAU'S APPEAL TO AGRICULTURISTS, VITICULTURISTS AND HORTICULTURISTS OF THE WORLD

Laborious phalanx, to whom I have the honour to belong by my birth, I come now towards you to raise my voice in favour of a great invention which will be, if you understand me, one of the great factors of the resurrection and prosperity of the whole world, as it means the intensifying of the production of the earth, the increasing of crops in considerable proportions, and minimising as much as possible the manual labour appertaining to culture and the economising of the immense sums of money which are being spent annually for fertilizers and replacing them by this new apparatus wherein are condensed all the forces of nature. That is to say: The land magnetism, telluric currents, the electricity of the floating air and that carried by the clouds, the sun, the wind, the rain, and even by the frost, forces which are captured and transformed into energetic electricity by this apparatus which carries them to the soil in a FEEBLE AND CONTINUOUS MANNER, and which renders it free from the microbes which attack the Seeds and Plants.

(Signed) J. CHRISTOFLEAU.

5

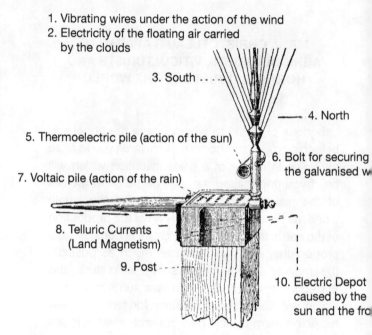

1. Vibrating wires under the action of the wind
2. Electricity of the floating air carried by the clouds
3. South . . . .
4. North
5. Thermoelectric pile (action of the sun)
6. Bolt for securing the galvanised w
7. Voltaic pile (action of the rain)
8. Telluric Currents (Land Magnetism)
9. Post
10. Electric Depot caused by the sun and the fro

ELECTROCULTURE

Electroculture is a method of applying atmospheric electricity to the fertilization of plant life, and has, during the past few years, developed to such an extent that it is today being practised in many of the countries of the world, viz.: France, England, Canada, Germany, Switzerland, Italy, Belgium, Denmark, Sweden, etc. Its success has been so marked that there are upwards of a million apparatus in use in these countries and its application is extending as its benefits become better known.

6

The discoverer of this process is a well-known French scientist—Mr. J. Christofleau—who devoted years of research to the development and application of his process, and the apparatus, which he finally perfected and patented throughout the world, is the result of his efforts.

The apparatus referred to is illustrated on previous page.

DESCRIPTION

Terrestrial Magnetism and Telluric Currents.— The apparatus must be firmly placed on a post at least 20 feet from the ground, with the horizontal pointer pointing direct magnetic South, and the perpendicular pointer to the sky.

No. 1. **Atmospheric Electricity.—** The currents with which the atmosphere is impregnated are captured by means of a perpendicular pointer, and the aerial wires of the apparatus, which serve as a conductor, by which means the positive atmospheric electricity is passed to the negative currents in the earth.

The horizontal pointer, which is pointing direct South, captures the terrestrial magnetism and telluric currents which surround the apparatus.

No. 2. **The Sun's Action.—** Inside the casing of the apparatus are ridges, and outside are flanges corresponding with the thinnest parts of the casing. When the apparatus is placed in position on the post, with the pointer direct South, the rising sun naturally strikes the eastern facet of the apparatus. The flanges on the outer portion of the

7

casing, serve to deflect the rays of the sun from the thin part of the casing to the thick ridges. These flanges also being exposed to the wind, cool the portion of the casing to which they are attached. The resultant difference in temperatures causes an electric "Depot," or store, due to the metallic particles. The same action takes place later on in the afternoon on the third facet, or western side, of the apparatus, thus DURING THE WHOLE DAY THE SUN CREATES AN ELECTRIC DEPOT IN THE WHOLE APPARATUS.

Thermo Pile.—Attached to the lower portion of the stem of the apparatus is a tube, which consists of two pieces of metal—one being copper and the other zinc, joined together by two solderings, and connected to the main stem, so that one of the solderings is exposed to the heat of the sun, while the other, being underneath, is shaded from its rays. This forms or generates an electric current from the copper to the zinc, that is, a negative and positive current, which is from there transmitted to that portion of the apparatus to which the zinc is attached.

The whole becomes a thermo electric magazine, and is brought about by the action of the sun's rays, and a contact of the zinc and the copper metals.

The Effect of Cold and Frost.—Cold and frost both engender electricity, due to the difference of temperatures transmitted to the walls or casing of the apparatus in the same manner as described in the preceding paragraph, under the heading of "The Sun's Action."

Effect of Wind.—The wind when blowing through the aerial wires causes them to vibrate and capture the positive electricity with which the air is charged.

Effect of the Rain.—On the top of the apparatus is a zinc saucer to which is riveted a copper plate; the very contact of these two metals alone is sufficient in itself to form an electric "Depot," or store, and, moreover, the saucer forms a receptacle for moisture caused either from the humidity of the atmosphere, the rain, the frost, or the dew.

This action on the zinc and copper saucer converts it into a voltaic battery. The apparatus itself being metallic and placed on a high post is cold and naturally serves to draw the moisture from the atmosphere. All this electrical energy gathered by the apparatus is the positive electricity of the atmosphere, which is transmitted to the soil by means of the galvanised wire.

The galvanised wire in the soil is directed in a straight line direct magnetic North for any distance required. This serves to capture the magnetic land currents. It is the combination of positive electricity from the atmosphere and the negative electricity from the earth which causes continual flux and reflux of natural electricity in the soil. This current destroys all the insects and parasites which attack plant life by the very fact that the vibrations caused are proportionately greater than the vibrations of the insects themselves.

Chemical transformations are formed, which will give to vegetation the fertilising elements and nitrogenous products which are necessary to the nourishment and development of plant life.

NOTES BY MR. JUSTIN CHRISTOFLEAU

As far back as 1749 Abbe Nollet who seems to be the first scientist who had noted the effects of electricity on vegetation, announced that electricity contributed to the EVAPORATION OF THE SOIL, facilitated the germination of seeds and increased the quickness of the ascension of the sap in vegetation.

In 1783 Abbe Bertholon not only made known the role of atmospheric electricity on vegetation in one of his works, but made its practical application with an "electro-vegetometre" which he invented.

At a much later period, a Russian scientist, Spechnoff, perfected the Electro-vegetometre, invented by Abbe Bertholon, and noted an over-production of 62 per cent. for oats, 56 per cent. for wheat, 34 per cent. for linseed. Mr. Spechnoff, furthermore, has found that the composition of the soil is modified by the action of the currents.

Towards the end of last century Brother Paulin, the Director of the Agricultural Institute of Beauvais, invented a new apparatus, the "Geomagnetifere," which gave wonderful results, especially as regards Grapes, which were richer in sugar and alcohol; their maturity was more hastened and more regular.

It is shown by all the experiments made to this day by scientists that the lands which were submitted to electricity have given crops that are more than one-third, double and even treble, according to the effectiveness of the apparatus and to the care given to its installation, and, moreover, that those crops are preserved from the microbes, the parasites and the epidemic diseases which are the ruination of agriculturists, those microbes, etc., being destroyed by electricity.

In order that I should not be accused of invoking the testimony of scientists who are long dead, it is pleasant for me to record the irrefutable testimony of experiments made with my apparatus by a number of persons of good repute who are actually living, who can be questioned, and whose experiments have been, in some cases, certified to by an officer of the Municipality.

J.C.

INSTALLATION INSTRUCTIONS

1.—Fix the apparatus firmly on the top of a 25ft. post, and make secure with a wooden peg in the hole on the southern facet of the apparatus.

2.—Bury the post 5ft. and face the pointer of the apparatus direct South (magnetic), and the head of the apparatus magnetic North. This is absolutely essential, as the entire functioning of the apparatus depends on this. (See page 14).

3.—Tar the top of the post which is inserted into the apparatus, and also the 5ft. of the post which is buried in the ground.

4.—Attach No. 12 gauge soft pliable galvanised iron wire to the bolt between the washer and the apparatus by a single "eye" loop and wind the end tightly around the main "down" wire for 6in.; then solder the end to make good contact. (See Fig. D. page 14).

5.—Insulate the main wire with 4 orb. porcelain insulators down the side of the post, care being taken that the wire is kept taut. (See Figs. A. and B. page 14).

6.—Use three stays, or "Guy" wires," to prevent the post from swaying in a heavy wind.

7.—Bury the wire 10 inches deep in a straight furrow, running from the post in a line direct magnetic North to the end of the strip of land which is to be electrified. In cases where the ground is to be ploughed, the wire must be buried at least four inches deeper than the depth of the plough. (See page 14).

8.—Use a double insulator, similar to those used for wireless aerials, at the base of the post under the ground, where the main wire turns at right angles from the post along the furrow. The wire is threaded through the insulator, which is attached to the base of the post by three short strands of strong wire. After the main wire has been correctly laid and fixed at each end, i.e., at the bolt of the apparatus and the peg at the northern extremity of the field, the short strands of wire holding the insulator at the base of the post are then twisted, or "twitched" up, as taut as possible, thus making the main wire in the furrow and down the post tight. (See page 14).

9.—Where the wire is cut off at the northern boundary, it is twisted firmly around a peg in the ground and the end of the wire is buried 18 inches.

10.—When establishing the correct direction for the furrow with a compass, it should be placed on a piece of dry board and never directly on the ground or within close proximity to any iron matter or wire, etc., as the earth currents and iron will influence the compass.

11.—The successful working of the apparatus depends entirely on the precise direction of the pointer of the apparatus being South (magnetic) and the underground wire being direct magnetic North.

12.—It is necessary to use dry timber for the post on which the apparatus is fixed, as green timber is apt to warp and thus throw the point of the apparatus out of direction.

13.—It is advisable to test the direction of the pointer from time to time in case the post has twisted. A good method for doing this is to drive two wooden pegs into the post, about 5 feet apart from each other, in a line directly under the pointer; the points thus being kept in an exact line. It is then easy to test the direction of the pointer by looking upwards from the bottom peg to the top point to see if all three are still in line; if not, it is necessary to re-set the apparatus with a good compass.

14.—Care must be taken to remove any roots or stones which lie in the course of the furrow.

15.—The wire must not be wound around the insulators on the post, but passed down the side and made fast to the insulator by means of a piece of light gauge 'tie' wire. (See Fig. B).

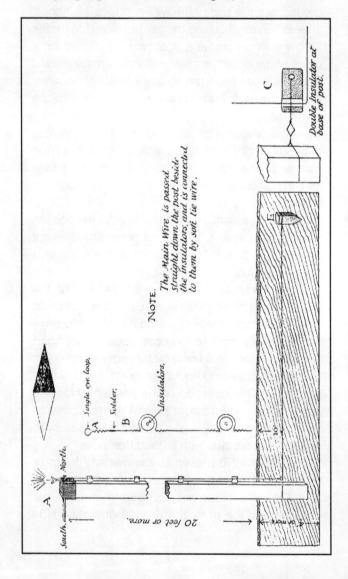

APPLICATION TO VINES PROVIDED WITH WIRES

The electrifying of vines that are on wires is very simple, and is considerably helped by the wires which are themselves charged with electricity.

As the apparatus influences a strip of ground 14ft. wide, if the rows of vines are 14ft. or less apart, it is advisable to place the post with the apparatus on it at the Southern end, equidistant between the rows, and run the wire in a straight furrow down the centre of the rows to a point direct North (magnetic) from the apparatus.

In cases where the rows are more than 14ft. apart, the apparatus can be placed at the Southern end of each row, and the wire directed in a furrow running North and within a few feet of the butts of the vines.

As a second method of applying the apparatus to a row of vines (See diagram on page 16). The main wire from the Apparatus may be attached to the top wire of the trellis, provided that the wire is of a suitable nature, i.e., 12 or 12½ gauge, soft and pliable, galvanised iron wire, and droppers of the same gauge wire are attached (see diagram on page 16).

The dropper wire is to protrude for 16 inches above the main top trellis wire, then passed in a perpendicular direction down, and buried 18 inches into the ground.

Of the two methods, the former is the most advisable. In both cases, it is essential, of course, that the rows of vines run direct South-North (magnetic).

Application to Vines on Wires.

6 m, 25.

NOTE

As the electricity goes well beyond the end where the wire has been cut off, and in order to prevent this escape into a neighbouring field, a barrage can be easily established by burying one peg at each extremity and fixing the same gauge wire and at the same depth as the main wire, 6ft. from the Northern Boundary.

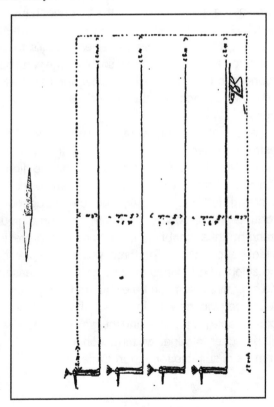

FOR VINES RUNNING EAST AND WEST

Erect posts 20ft. above the ground to carry the apparatus at the Southern end of the vineyard; the posts 14ft. apart, with an 8ft. strainer post directly opposite, each apparatus at the North end of the field.

Connect number 12 or 12½ gauge soft and pliable galvanised iron wire to the apparatus, insulating it down the post for 13ft.; then connect (using insulators) with the strainer post on the Northern boundary, the wire passing over each trellis to be connected to a dropper of the same gauge wire, but droppers to be left 16 inches above the aerial wire and buried 18 inches in the ground (see diagram on page 81).

The effect of the apparatus on vines, apart from destroying insects, parasites, etc., by the very fact that the vibrations caused in the ground are higher than the vibrations of the insects themselves, is to create fertilising matter, and the nitrogenous products which gives to each vine prodigious strength, thus enabling it to successfully resist rnildew and odium. For three years the spraying and sulphuring of vines may be greatly decreased, and after five years can be eliminated altogether.

Electrified vines will increase the crop in a considerable proportion, and the grapes themselves will be richer in sugar and in alcohol, thus making them more suitable for export trade.

APPLICATION TO A ROW OF TREES

When a row of trees is to be electrified, no matter what its length may be, provided that it runs direct South-North, the apparatus is placed on a post 20ft. above the ground at the Southern end of the trees, and as is the case with vines, if the rows of trees are 14ft. or less apart, place the post with the apparatus equidistant between the rows at the Southern end, and run the wire in the furrow down the middle of the rows in a direct line to a point on the Northern boundary. If the rows are more than 14ft. apart, place the apparatus and post near the head of the row, and run the wire in the furrow North from it, passing within a few feet of the butts of the trees.

Trees treated in this manner will be more vigorous and make quicker growth, and the fruit produced is larger, sweeter, and will ripen two weeks in advance of the non-electrified trees. The fruit contains more alcohol, and will keep better, and thus be more suitable for export trade.

Cereals will contain more carbo-hydrate.

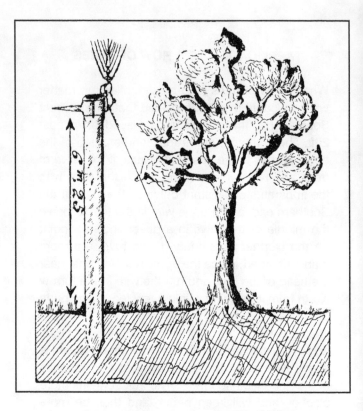

APPLICATION TO ISOLATED TREES

Electrification of a Single Tree.—It is very easy to electrify one single tree. The apparatus is placed within three feet of it, the tree being North of the apparatus. The galvanised wire is buried 15 or 16 inches at the base of the tree, and a few buckets of water (preferably rain water) are thrown where the wire is buried. After a few months the tree will gain a new vigor, and, if it is ailing, it will throw out new shoots and will rapidly improve.

ELECTROCULTURE
By GEORGE BLANCHARD

SCIENTIFIC CHAT

The omission of a correction in the text of a pamphlet makes me state that electricity killed "ALL" the parasites of the soil. This word "ALL" is misleading at least in what concerns electricity of low voltage such as supplied by the Christofleau apparatus, for currents able to kill all parasites would also destroy vegetation.

Atmospheric electricity, like all currents of low intensity, destroys cryptogamic diseases of vegetation which is already a great point. Currents of 110 and 220 volts are more deadly to plant parasites than low currents, but THEY ARE NOT innocuous to the plant itself.

If a current of 110 volts is conveyed to the soil during several hours per day it can, as shown by Mr. Breton, exercise a slightly favourable influence on vegetation, but the Hungarian Professor Kovessi showed in 1912 that the same current applied CONTINUOUSLY was absolutely detrimental to vegetation which it eradicated altogether.

I intentionally pass over all the other methods of applying electricity to cultivation (i.e., INDUCTION CURRENTS, HIGH TENSION ELECTRIC LIGHT, ULTRA VIOLET RAYS, etc.). They are all mentioned in the minutes of the First Congress of Electroculture, that was held at Rheims in 1912, under the presidency of Professor Armand Gauthier. They have for me an experimental value certainly, but they are less interesting than the method which I am about to relate.

Proofs are forthcoming daily in favour of this theory which is THE ONLY RATIONAL METHOD of applying electricity to the life and to the diseases of plants, of human beings and of animals, and this formula will purvey the whole of the electrotherapy and electroculture, i.e., THE CONTINUOUS FLOW OF A CURRENT OF LOW INTENSITY.

The recent scientific work of A. Lumiere tells us of organic liquid composed of celloids whose grains called by him "micelles" or "electrical granules," are charged with contrary electricity inside and outside. However we view this world of infinitely "smalls" animated by continuous movement due to the attraction of the contrary poles, and to repulsions of identical poles, and we see ourselves forced from deduction to deduction, to consider the electrical fluid as the true vital fluid regulating the circulation of the sap like that of blood and performing its task of exchange in favouring all the exchanges and the elaboration of the indispensable products to the maintenance of life.

Although they are in the domain of hypothesis, it is well to meditate upon the conceptions of Chardin and Lumiere, for they are not contrary to any scientific principle and no one has, so far, doubted them.

Electricity is so weak that it almost escapes our investigations. Chardin easily concludes it is ridiculous to come to its help with powerful currents.

22

Tomato Plants grown by
the Electroculture process

If it is stated that electricity has caused cures by suggestion to human beings, one cannot have such pretention as regards an animal or a plant.

I was therefore already cognisant of this method and convinced of the bad effects and the uselessness of the CURRENTS WHICH GAVE SHOCKS when by chance I became acquainted with the process of electroculture as practised by Mr. Christofleau.

I was immediately attracted by the way the electricity acted on vegetation, showing thus the greatest analogy with its actions on human beings and animals; analogy between the feeble current applied in PUERICULTURE, and the feeble current applied to the culture of plants; analogy between the human and veterinary therapeutical action, and the curing of the diseases of vegetation—analogy between the fatal action of intense currents on human beings, and animals and that no less fatal action of those currents on plant life.

I would therefore have lacked curiosity if I had not studied electroculture comparatively, as it touched so much on the electro-therapy which I practised.

This is how I became, therefore, a fervent disciple of electroculture. It is not through candour I became an apostle of the Christofleau method, and my convictions repose on the experiments I have made personally.

Abbe Nollett, Secretary of the Academy of Science, Berthollon, Paulin, Spechnoff, Becquorel and the great Marcelin Berthelot, were not hallucinated persons. Have not the two last mentioned shown the INDISPUTABLE INFLUENCE OF ELECTRICITY ON

THE FIXATION OF THE NITROGEN BY THE SOIL AND THE PLANTS? Is it not known already that under the influence of the current the nitrification of the soil is produced, GIVING BIRTH TO THE NITRATES, TO CYANAMIDE which are excellent fertilising nitrogenous elements? When a plant is submitted to absolute darkness not only does it not develop, but rapidly perishes, whereas, if a feeble electric current is passed into the vase which contains it, the plant will not only develop itself, but will reach perfect fructification. In order to explain this fact, Mr. Basty stated at the Congress of Rheims that the artificial current replaced in this case, the SOLAR ELECTRICITY WHICH IS INDISPENSABLE TO VEGETATION.

ONE FINDS IN THE ELECTRIFIED PLOTS OF LAND DOUBLE THE HUMIDITY OF THAT IN THE COMPARATIVE PLOTS AND THIS IS EXPLAINED BY THE LIBERATION OF MOLECULES OF WATER DUE TO THE CHEMICAL REACTION OF ELECTROLYSIS AS SHOWN BY THE INCONTESTIBLE SUPERIORITY OF ELECTROCULTURE OVER THE CHEMICAL MANURES IN TIMES OF DROUGHT.

The above scientific statements can only interest agriculturists by exposing to them the practical results obtained.

I will not refer to the experiments made at Metz by the French Government, for the results of these experiments have been communicated to the inventor himself and not to me. I could again speak of the marvelous results obtained in Belgium in the culture of beetroot with the chemical analysis attached, and also of the results made known to me by the Society of Electroculture of Switzerland, and of those results obtained in foreign countries. All those results will be published later on. For the time being my readers would be quite correct in stating those countries are far away, and it is therefore difficult to control those experiments. Let us speak, therefore, of the French experiments exclusively. Must one tell the sceptics and the incredulous that two years successively a grower has been able to crop two beautiful crops of beetroot, and one knows how beetroot drains the soil, so much so that it is generally grown in the same soil but EVERY THIRD YEAR.

One of my correspondents, Mr. Fernand Frison, 56 Awvingtstreet, Cambrai, told me of a fact which is still more extraordinary. "A field of rye was cut when 22 inches high and given to cattle: the rye grew again and had beautiful ears. The second time it was cut I noted some of the shoots were 4ft. 6in. High. The stalks and the ears of this second crop were more beautiful than those in the neighbouring field which had not been cut when green." Please note that usually one never cuts two crops of rye.

On the 16th August, 1925, I gave a conference at the Agricultural Comice of L'Isle-sur-le-Doubs and to which the professors of agriculture of that region attended. During my conference I cited the following results, which were obtained at the place named "Croix de Mission," on a plot of land that was electrified. The oats cropped there have grown on an average 4ft. and had 54 grains to the ear. On the comparative crop which was not electrified the average height of the oats was 32 inches, and the ears contained but 29 grains. It is necessary to state that the crop of oats for that year was somewhat deficient, and the agriculturists who were present admired the results of the crop that was electrified and rendered homage to facts.

A Border of Parsley

APPLICATION OF ELECTRICITY TO PLANT LIFE
By Mr. G. Blanchard

The main object of "ELECTROCULTURE" is to make known to Agriculturists some of the forces of nature which can be utilised to advantage.

A French inventor—Mr. J. Christofleau—has demonstrated that there is no need for manures to fertilise the soil, and that nature—and nature alone—is rich enough in itself to provide the necessary nourishment to plant life. The sun's rays, rain, nitrogen of the air, atmospheric electricity carried by clouds, all these elements can be utilised to take the place of manures.

If manure is used to intensify the growth, it must not be assumed that the chemical products have a direct influence on vegetation. The facts are:—

All chemical bodies, which decompose, give forth an electric current, and it is to this electric current which is due to the decomposition of manures in the ground which gives to vegetation the necessary fluid for the intense development of the plant.

The elements from the atmosphere bring far more nourishment to the plants than the soil itself and strengthen our statement that if chemical fertilisers intensify the production, it is because their decomposition in the soil PRODUCES AN ELECTRIC CURRENT WHICH STRENGTHENS THAT OF THE ATMOSPHERE.

The capture of atmospheric electricity to the benefit of culture is, therefore, an invention of the greatest importance and only sceptics will refuse to make use of this natural force which costs nothing.

In order to intensify the crops one cannot expect the forces of nature unaided to fertilise the soil. They must be captured, drained and directed where they are required, and this is what Mr. Christofleau's apparatus will do. The results of electrifying crops are very marked:

1. In a field that was not manured nor irrigated, but influenced by Mr. Christofleau's apparatus, oats measuring 5ft. 6in. were cropped. In another field the oats grew to 7ft., and were oî excellent quality.

2. Trefoil grown in the same conditions measured 5ft. 3in.

3 . Potatoes were grown under the same condition, the plants were 6ft. 3in. high, each plant carried 30 to 35 tubers, whose weight varied from 1lb. 1oz. to 2lb. 2oz. each, and they were of exceptional quality.

4. Vines that were badly attacked by phyloxera were cured and rejuvenated to such an extent that after three years treatment by the apparatus they were heavily laden with enormous bunches of very sweet grapes. (Here it may be mentioned that all grapes grown with the assistance of electroculture are much sweeter and have a much richer flavour, besides being richer in alcohol.)

5. Carrots grew to a length of 19 inches, beetroot to 18 inches and nearly 17 inches in circumference, and tomatoes, French beans, asparagus, artichokes, and celery grew proportionately.

6. As regards fruit trees, the results are truly

astounding. An old pear tree, so old that it hardly had any bark left on the trunk and having but few leaves, produced an abundance of pears as the result of electroculture, some weighing as much as 1lb. each.

The above are only a few illustrations which go to show what can be done without the use of manures. The Christofleau apparatus not only captures the atmospheric electricity, but also forms an association of the positive electricity of the atmosphere with the magnetism of the earth, the telluric currents.

The heat of the sun, the rain, the wind and even frost all come together in turn to determine or form in the apparatus a function which transforms itself into electricity. All these combined actions produce in plants an extraordinary vital energy. The apparatus which makes its own electricity at no cost whatever, and will last for a man's lifetime.

Long before Mr. Christofleau, attempts of the same kind were made, but the apparatus were very imperfect, and the cost was too great for practical application.

The Christofleau apparatus is a magnetic mass which is placed on a post, the steel point is turned toward the South, and the head toward the North. The point captures the magnetism of the earth, the electric currents, whilst the electricity of the air is captured by the aerials which are on top of the apparatus and are pointed skywards. By a distribution of ridges and flanges the sun, the cold, the frost, the wind and the rain supply their contingent of electric forces which is distributed to the soil by means of a galvanised wire.

The many Parasites which attack plants are destroyed and the beneficial effects of the electricity always travelling from the South to North, from the chemical transformation which gives to vegetation the necessary elements for its nourishment and development.

Once the apparatus is fixed there is no need to interfere with it, and it remains there indefinitely, and the first expense has been made once and for all time, and the cost of manuring is minimised, for the soil contains it. The results will go on increasing, that is to say, that the second year and the years following it will be better than the first.

The ears of the crop will be larger and fuller, the leaves of vegetables, fruit trees, vines and other vegetation will begin to be thicker, larger, and greener, the fruit will be larger and more numerous, the vegetables, such as potatoes, tomatoes, beans, etc., will be much larger and more abundant.

But this is only the first result which goes on increasing until the fifth or sixth year when the soil, which is then much richer, causes the vegetation to be more constant and more abundant and richer in useful elements, such as starch, sugar and alcohol. The fruit is sweeter and the flavour is much more pronounced. There can never be any failure, providing the apparatus is correctly pointing toward the needle of the compass—that is, South-North.

We wish to overcome the scepticism and the prejudice which growers often manifest to new scientific processes, and we do not anticipate much difficulty in demonstrating to them the many advantages of Mr. Christofleau's discovery. To the incredulous and the timid growers, we assure them that even a modest trial will convince them of the extraordinary value of the feeble atmospheric and magnetic currents to vegetation.

We simply ask them to make a trial of two to six apparatus on their land, taking care to make the comparison alongside where the apparatus has been placed, i.e., alongside where the wire has been buried. The result for the first year will clearly and effectively demonstrate the value of the method, and the increase of the yield will largely repay for the expense of the trial. The next year, pleased with the marvellous results the experimenters will become fully convinced of the efficacy of the invention.

The atmospheric electricity captured by the Christofleau apparatus accumulates in the soil until it is saturated with it. The first year the overproduction repays largely, as stated before, for the cost of the installation, and this increase goes on year by year until the fifth or sixth year; from then on the crops, etc., will remain stationary and of constant regularity as regards abundance and the exceptional quality. The soil will have reached its maximum of capacity of production and will remain at that. They attain a very high yield, of ten up to 100 per cent. or more, in comparison with crops grown by the aid of artificial manure.

The ravages of drought are greatly minimised, and we will explain the reason why: As it is necessary to have water or rain to decompose the fertilisers in the soil, and thus supply to the plants the necessary current to their vitality, the Christofleau apparatus supplies this current slowly, but continuously, and, therefore it supplements rain just as it supplements fertilisers. Likewise, vegetation growing in soil which is electro-magnetic is immuned from rotting by heavy rains, as the germs of rot cannot develop when in contact with the electric currents. (N.B.— This should, therefore, eliminate "rust" altogether.) It has been noticed that influenced crops resist much more victoriously the effects of frost. The proof of the accumulation of electricity in the soil was signalled to me by a reputed electrician who, after reading my articles on electroculture, applied electric currents of feeble intensity to an ailing aspidestras by means of a weak electric current of only a few "milliamperes" in the soil where the plant was. Five days after stopping the current he noticed the soil had retained all the electricity he had introduced to it, and the plant had become greener under the beneficial influence of this phenomenon.

It bas been pointed out to me that industrial electric currents could produce the same results as the electricity which was captured by the Christofleau apparatus. This comparison was made and the advantage of atmospheric electricity was manifest: the industrial currents not attaining the yield given by electro-magnetic process. Does it mean to say that the constitution and the quality of the fluid are different in the atmospheric current and the industrial current? No, certainly not. But there is a point on which we essentially and immediately insist. It is on the extraordinary difference which exists between the effects of the currents of a FEEBLE INTENSITY, but of continuous application, and those of intense currents, but of limited application. Experiments have been made by using currents of 110 volts during a limited time, and renewing the application every day. Such electrification has never been able to show an increase of more than between 25 per cent. to 30 per cent. in comparison made with comparative plots. With the Christofleau process its beneficial effects rebound not only on the general development of the plants themselves, but also, and especially so, on the increase of the yield and on the size and the exceptional quality of the cereals, vegetables, fruit, tubers, vines, etc., which become richer in useful elements such as starch, sugar, alcohol, etc., and increase in not merely 25 per cent. to 30 per cent., but of 100 per cent. and 200 per cent., and of ten more. To what can this crushing superiority in favour of the Christofleau process be attributed? Undoubtedly to these three essential factors:

1. The feeble intensity of the current.

2. To its continuous application.

3. Certainly to its magnetic action which could not be supplied by industrial electricity. All agriculturists know the beneficient effect of a steady if even light rain as compared with heavy and short showers of rain. The atmospheric current, the magnetic effluvium cost nothing, nor do the currents supplied by the Christofleau apparatus, which are supplied

by the sun, rain, clouds, wind and frost. There is absolutely no doubt as to the beneficial effects of atmospheric electricity in vegetation. Several scientists have proved it. Abbe Nollet in 1749, Abbe Bertholon in 1783, and a little later on Spechnoff, a Russian scientist, demonstrated the influence of electricity on vegetation, and by means of his process Spechnoff showed an increase of yield of 100 per cent. The idea was never abandoned, and if the predecessors of Mr. Christofleau could not put their ideas into practice, it was due to the fact that their apparatus were too complicated, susceptible to change of temperature, of a high cost, and could not be used economically. The success of the inventor, Mr. Christofleau, is in having realised a maximum yield, to have accumulated in his apparatus, besides the atmospheric current, the currents produced by the sun, the rain, the clouds, the wind, and the frost, and to have made an apparatus which is very strong, practicable, not susceptible to the vagaries of the temperature, which will last forever, and which does not require any attention or maintaining. The proximity of a wireless plant is no detriment to Electroculture, nor is it necessary for the land to be treated to be flat, as it may be undulating, and have several depressions. BUT ONE FACT IS VERY IMPORTANT, AND THAT IS THAT THE WIRE BE DIRECTED DIRECTLY NORTH BY THE COMPASS. The only detriment might be when trees are within, say, 100 yards to the South of the apparatus, for the reason that the electrical currents which invariably travel South to North would

Field of Potatoes grown by
the Electroculture process.
Height, 6ft. 3in. Number of Tubers
to each plant 30 to 35.
Weight of each Tuber
from 1lb. 1oz. to 2lb. 2oz.

be intercepted and would consequently interfere with the efficiency of the apparatus. In such cases, though, the effect would not be nullified; it would take a comparatively longer period to attain its object. Any obstructions, such as trees or buildings, to the North, however, would not influence the effect in any way.

Electroculture bas been highly praised by many scientists, who have given the inventor much encouragement, and today ranks as one of the most important discoveries of the age.

G.B.

The set of nine poles erected at Mr. C. E. Pope's nursery, St. Martins. On the top of each of these is placed one of the Apparatus.

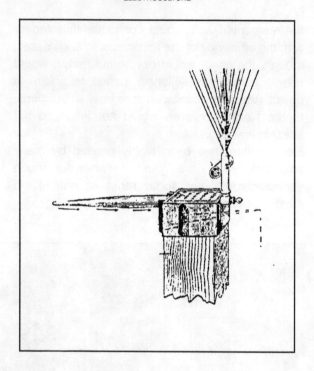

A close up view of the Apparatus.

OPINION OF SCIENTISTS

Extract from the "Electro Revue," of January,
1921. Article Written and Signed by the Celebrated
Electrician, Dr. Foreau de Courmelles.

"The idea of increasing the yield of agriculture by
the use of electricity, that is to say, by employing
this fluid to activate plant growth, is not new.

"Some rather successful experiments were made
in the eighteenth century when science made great
progress. The Abbes Nollet, Bertholon and Sans
made experiments during that century. I will quote
this passage of a conference which I made on the
28th of February, 1893, at the annual fete of the
Horticultural Society of Picardie, at Amiens:—'If the
plant is neurasthenic, that is to say, devoid of vigour,
although it is not actually ailing, the electricity will be
of great benefit to it, just as it is to human beings.'

"An experiment was made on two identical fields,
which were planted with the same vegetation, by
means of metallic chains which traversed one of the
fields and by which oxydised electric currents were
formed. The growth of the plants on the electrified
field was more considerable than on the other field.
Knowing the happy results I have obtained by the
application of electricity to human diseases, I was
not astonished, therefore, at this result. To revert
back, therefore, to the method to be applied to
ailing and neurasthenic plants and human beings,
the remedy is found, viz., the electrification of
morbid vegetation.

"Abbe Bertholon has demonstrated this cure a long time ago. Many experiments with electricity have been made since the 18th Century on vegetation. In this era when, due to under production, the cost of living is so dear, any suggestion that will increase the yield of our natural resources should be published, encouraged and put to practical use. It is, therefore, pleasant for me to discuss the work of one of the readers of the 'Electro Revue,' Mr. Justin Christofleau, who knows and quotes the work of his predecessors, Abbes Nollet and Bertholon. Abbe Nollet, who was the tutor of Louis XVI., announced to the world that electricity contributed to THE EVAPORATION OF THE SOIL, it facilitated the germination of the seeds and increased the ascending acceleration of the sap in vegetation.

"Abbe Bertholon, who also treated human diseases by means of electricity, invented the 'Electro-vegetometre,' in order to test its action on plant life. In 1900 Brother Paulin, the Director of the Agricultural Society of Beauvais, carried out some very successful experimcnts at Montbrisson. Finally, Mr. Grandeau has established the fact that the nitrification of the products of the soil through vegetation was due to the atmospheric electricity.

"The nitrogenous products take from the floating air and from the electric fluid, the elements of their transformations; this is undeniable, and is being used industrially today.

"Being well conversant with the above facts and by following the laws of terrestrial magnetism, Mr. Justin Christofleau has invented and put to practical use a very simple apparatus, which captures the telluric currents, those terrestrial currents which direct the needle of the compass to indicate the North and the South. This apparatus is placed on a wooden post 20ft. high (at least) and is placed strictly as per the direction of the needle of the compass, the boreal and austral parts carry the antennae North and South so that the magnetic current travelling from North to South is captured in its passage by the antennae of the apparatus. A galvanised wire conducts this electricity in the soil. The floating air which is electrified, electrifies also the point of the antennae and this electricity which follows the same course as the terrestrial current adds its action in the depths of the soil. The result is excellent, and this is not surprising and there is nothing left but to propagate the invention. This double electricity has no limit, one can thus gather the terrestrial and aerial fluids for miles and miles and double the production without increasing manual labour."

A few Strawberries

Haricot Beans
Grown with   Grown by Electroculture
manure.   Process without Manure.

OFFICIAL REPORTS

Experiments made at the Institution of Agriculture
of Metz with the Electroculture apparatus.

FRENCH REPUBLIC

The Director of the Agriculture Station of Metz,
                    Metz, August 5th, 1921.

To Mr. J. Christofleau,
In answer to your letter of July 26th, I have the

honour to enclose herewith the reports on the results of the trials made with your apparatus by Mr. Sabatier, PRINCIPAL CHEMIST, at the Station of Agriculture of Metz.

Please accept, Sir, my salutations.

(Signed) The Director of the Agriculture Station of Metz.

REPORT OF MR. SABATIER
Engineer of Agriculture and Chief Chemist at the Station of Agriculture of Metz. Experiment of Electroculture with the Christofleau Apparatus.

1. On Fruit Trees

We have observed a more intense vegetation by the action of the apparatus on an ailing apricot tree. The disease was due to a mushroom parasite which has completely disappeared, and during the month of August we noticed numerous and very vigorous new shoots. The fructification was forcibly mediocre for all the fruit trees had been attacked by a black frost of 6 degrees when the trees were in bloom.

2. On Vegetables

A field of French Beans was divided in two parts. One was submitted to the actions of the apparatus of electroculture, the other served as the comparative plot, the manuring of the two parcels was identical. Under the action of the Christofleau process the French Beans resisted the dry weather; the growth always remained regular, and one could notice a uniform growth on all the influenced parcel. The comparative parcel could not resist the intense drought which took place in the month of July. The stalks of the beans on that parcel became completely yellow, and the crop was considerably lessened. The parcel of land where the Christofleau apparatus were installed produced THREE TIMES the crop of the comparative parcel.

Those experiments merit the attention of the agriculturists, arboriculturists, viticulturists and horticulturists. However, they must be persevered with for two or three years on different cultures in order to show their action on vegetation in general and on the fructification of fruit trees in particular.

OPINION OF THE PRESS

Extract from the "Agriculture de Touraine" Newspaper, 26th May, 1921

AN IMMENSE PROGRESS IN AGRICULTURE — ELECTROCULTURE

The work of scientists and the experience acquired by them as the years go on has demonstrated that when a calamity affects mankind, Nature comes to the aid of humanity with some natural help or other in order to combat this calamity.

The frightful cataclysm which has recently swept

all over the world has had a long sequence of very unfortunate consequences, and amongst those unfortunate consequences there is one which is particularly grave, as it affects millions of individuals who are crushed, so to speak, by its enormous weight.

This consequence is THE HIGH COST OF LIVING. It is necessary, therefore, to combat this evil. Many divers means have been suggested and so far, the results have been exceedingly meagre. There is only one way of remedying this evil. THE INTENSIFICATION OF THE PRODUCTION OF THOSE THINGS THAT ARE NECESSARY TO LIFE.

The problem, therefore, is this: TO INCREASE THE PRODUCTION OF THE SOIL, THUS LESSENING THE COST OF IMPORTATION, WHICH CRIPPLES THE RETURNS OF AGRICULTURISTS.

THE SOLUTION IS FOUND IN ELECTROCULTURE.

IN ELECTROCULTURE

Electroculture is an old science. For centuries past scientists had discovered that this mysterious force of electricity was connected to the life of men, of animals, and of plants, and having noted its effects on animated bodies, have applied it to the benefit of vegetation. Many inventors have applied electricity to the development of plants and they have all obtained impressive and conclusive results. It was, therefore, a long established fact that electricity influenced the life of plants and developed them, but no one had found the means and ways of applying this principle in a practical manner until one of our compatriots, an indefatigable searcher (who during the grave period of the war rendered many services to the National Defence) after many years of experimental work and trials has so effectively solved this difficulty by the surprising results he has obtained that he has patented a system of electroculture which is to agriculture what wireless telegraphy is to the aerial telegraphy of Chappe.

White Haricots from Spain,
Grown July, 1926—9ft. High.

Peas 7½ to 9ft. High, Grown June 1926.

Electroculture is born, and agriculture owes its genial application to Mr. Justin Christofleau. IN THE FUTURE THE NEED OF CHEMICAL MANURES TO FERTILISE OUR LAND WILL BE GREATLY MINIMISED. Hitherto, all the inventors had put forth different systems which were no doubt efficacious, but were inapplicable as they were too complicated. Mr. Christofleau has invented a small and simple apparatus which, placed at one end of a field, captures the atmospheric currents which it combines with the telluric currents, which coming in contact are carried by a galvanised wire to the soil wherein they deposit their beneficial effects, whereby they multiply in an incredible manner the quantity and quality of the crops.

47

"The Brisbane Daily Mail"
October 10th, 1926

WORLD FAMINE
Crop Shrinkage

London, Tuesday.—Sir Daniel Hall, Chief Scientific Adviser and Director-General of the Intelligence Dept. of the Ministry of Agriculture, speaking before the British Association, foreshadowed the spectre of a great famine when the world's wheat fields were unable to feed the multiplying peoples.

Sir Daniel said the good land was already short, necessitating dairy farming alternately with agriculture in Australia and South Africa. The world's wheat-eating population was increasing by 5,000,000 a year, necessitating the finding of 12,000,000 acres of additional land, whereas, on the contrary, there had been a shrinkage in acreage of many crops since the war.

The white peoples might be forced to teetotalism and vegetarianism, but the races omitting meat and alcohol in order to multiply themselves were the permanent slave types, designed to function like worker bees.

Agriculture had lost its best brains owing to the small returns yielded.

The flight from the land to the city was progressing everywhere. Over-population and unemployment were terrible realities, AND MANKIND'S ONLY HOPE WAS SCIENTIFICALLY INTENSIFYING THE CULTIVATION OF EXISTING LAND.

Extract from the '"Homme Libre"
Newspaper 20th February,1921
Article written by Mr. Fernand Hure

"If some one said to us: 'There is no more need of coal, of petrol, no need of lubricating oil to help the functioning of machinery in the factories; no more need of fertilisers for culture,' we would be inclined to think it a miracle. It is nevertheless a reality. At the village of La Queue-les-Yvelines, near the forest of Rambouillet we have seen Mr. Christofleau, an indefatigable worker belonging to this very rare elite, who works quietly and silently.

"Mr. Christofleau (who has also invented an aerial turbine capable of obviating the use of charcoal and which he presented to the French Government during the war), working on the laws of the terrestrial magnetism has invented an apparatus which captures the electricity of the air and spreads it in the soil where it contributes to the formation of nitrogenous products.

"His apparatus, which has been patented all over the world under the name of 'Electro-magnetic-terro Celestial,' is extremely simple, and its effect on vegetation is really marvellous. The cereals, vegetables, vines, fruit trees, grow with an extraordinary vigour by assimilating rapidly the nutritive substances of the soil. This means we are on the eve of a total revolution of our present methods of culture. "Abbe Moreux, the Director of the Observatory of Bourges states that the apparatus will impart extraordinary yields to the plants that are submitted to its influence.

"The precious electric fluid can be used for miles and miles, forming practically an immense magnetic network within which, the malevolent microbes and parasites perish.

"Vines treated by Mr. Christofleau's process are immune from phyloxera and mildew.

"Is this not, therefore, a source of inestimable riches for agriculture? Mr. Christofleau has fulfilled his duty to mankind. We humbly fulfill ours by calling attention to his work."

Extract from "La Revue du Ciel"
Newspaper Article Written
by Abbe Moreux

"This problem is not new and amongst the experiments that have has been made to solve it, I must quote Abbe Nollet, who was the first to notice the influence of electricity on vegetation. In 1783 Abbe Bertholon noted the action of atmospheric electricity on vegetation in one of his works, but made a practical application of it by the aid of the 'Electro-vegetometre.'

"About 1900 Brother Paulin, Director of the Agriculture Institute of Beauvais, made successful experiments at Montbrisson, which created a great sensation. More recently still, Mr. Grandeau, the Agricultural Scientist has established the fact that electricity had a notable influence on the nitrification of the products of the soil through vegetation.

"Following upon the above stated experiments Mr. Christofleau who is also the inventor of an aerial turbine of a capacity of 15,000 horse-power, has invented an apparatus which he has named the 'Electro-magnetic-terro Celestrial,' which captures the electricity of the air in order to spread it in the soil where it contributes to the formation of nitrogenous products. It is of great importance to direct the apparatus SOUTH-NORTH, the steel pointer towards the SOUTH and the subterranean wire towards the NORTH. It is sufficient for the subterranean wire to be placed in the soil about two inches below the passage of the plough. The posts on which the apparatus is secured must be placed at a distance of 10ft.

"For some time now the use of Mr. Christofleau's apparatus has greatly developed, and it appears that everyone praises the invention which gives to the vegetation subjected to the influence of electricity thus captured, EXTRAORDINARY YIELDS. Our readers who are interested in agriculture will be grateful to us for having attracted their attention to this."

List of Newspapers that have Favourably Commented on the Christofleau Agriculture Process

"La Nature," 28th March, 1921.

"La Bonhomme Normand," 1st April, 1921.

"La Belgique Productrice," 1st April, HJ21.

"Le Sud Marocain," 7th April, 1921.

"La Vallée d'Aoste," 9th April, 1921.

"Le Paysan de France," 10th April, 1921.

"Le Revue Economique de Tours," 16th April, 1921.

"La Defence Agricole de la Bance et du Perche," June 4th, 1921.

"L'Union Catholique de Rodez," 16th August, 1921.

"Le Radical de Paris," 7th Septcmber, 1921.

"La Democratie Nouvelle," 30th July, 1922.

"Le Pionnier," June, 1922.

"Le Chasseur Français," February 22nd, 1923.

"L'Electricien," 15th April, 1923.

"Le Magasin Pittoresque," 15th April, 1923.

"Le Paysan de l'Yonne," 15th May, 1923.

"La Revue Mondiale," 15th May, 1923.

"Le Petit Inventeur," 12th June, 1923.

"L'Aube Nouvelle," 30th June, 1923.

"Le Soir de Bruxelles," 15th June, 1923.

"Le Pionnier," January, 1923.

"Almanach du Petit Parisien," June, 1924.

"L'Homme Libre," 23rd and 27th July, 1924.

"L'Excelsior," July, 1924.

"The Times" (Paris edition), 3rd August, 1924.

"Le Fermier," 11th August and 30th October, 1924.

"L'Indépendant de Rambouillet," 15th August, 1924.

"L'Industrie Naturelle Belge," 21st August, 1924.

"L'Almanach du Petit haut Marnais," 1925.

"L'Oeuvre," 2nd March, 1924.

"Le Petit Parisien," 2nd November, 1924.

"L'intransigeant," 3rd November, 1924 and 1st February, 1925. "Berlin Tageblatt," 16th November 1924.

"Le Matin d'Anvers," 20th November, 1924 and 28th December, 1924.

"The World Magazine," 22nd March, 1925.

"Lokal Auzeiger," 8th April, 1925.

"Der Blitz," 21st May, 1925.

"La Revue Mondiale," 15th July, 1925.

"The Popular Science Magazine," June, 1925.

"The Primary Producers' News," Sydney, January, 21, 1927.

"The Primary Producer," Perth, February 10, 1927.

"The Sunday Times," Perth, June 13, 20, 27, 1926.

"The Truth Newspaper," Perth, July 16, 1927.

"The West Australian," Perth, July 7, 1927.

"The Mirror," Perth, July 23, 1927.

"The Otago Daily Times," New Zealand, April, 1927.

"The Timaru Herald," New Zealand, April, 1927.

"The Lyttleton Press," New Zealand, March 5, 1927.

"The World's News," Sydney, January 15, 1927.

"The Recorder," South Australia, December 11, 1926.

MISCELLANEOUS NOTES

Instead of alternate crops in the wheat centres where the rainfall is small, fallowing must be carried on every second year. While the soil is resting, the apparatus is never idle, but is constantly depositing electricity and fertilising matter into the soil, and it still goes on with its work the following year while the crop is growing, thus functioning perpetually. After three years, crops can be cropped every year, providing the soil is allowed to rest for one year every fifth or sixth year.

It is evident there is not one man living today who can explain why electricity makes the plants grow, because we are here confronted with the great mystery of life-we can only notice the effects which electricity has upon vegetation. The plants are stronger, more healthy, more vigorous, more green; the crops yield more, the cars are bigger and fuller, vegetables and fruit larger, more hastened, more numerous. As for the chemical transformations which take place in the soil by the action of electricity, we must, as far as science is concerned in its present state, content ourselves to note the beneficial results and to profit thereby. If some day this mystery is explained so much the better.

1. By the reason of the changes of the electricity of the air with the electricity of the earth, they create vibrations which small insects cannot resist.

2. The plants assimilating the electricity are much more vigorous and will, later on, when the soil becomes more impregnated with electricity, resist more victoriously all the diseases and parasites that may attack them.

Germany has offered in vain 12 million francs for the world's right of Mr. Christofleau's apparatus.

When joining the ends of the wire it is advisable to splice them very tightly for about 15 or 16 inches, and to solder the ends so as to ensure no leakage.

The higher the post is above the ground, the better will be the results.

With the help of the agriculturists a new era of prosperity is rapidly approaching, and will shortly extend right through the Commonwealth.

Everything grown by electroculture is more healthful to human consumption and to the general health of the public.

A Beautiful Crop of Wheat

Cabbage
Measuring 11 feet in circumference

The wise and progressive agriculturist will readily recognise the virtues of the electroculture process, and will not waste any time in installing the apparatus.

Anything grown by the electroculture process is hastened, and consequently will have the benefit of an early market.

When a piece of land is to be electrified, the operation is very simple. By means of a compass, directions South-North are correctly established; this is most important, as the land magnetism travels South-North. The apparatus is then set with the pointer direct South, so as to capture the telluric currents, and the wire placed in the furrow direct North, thus capturing the land magnetism (earth currents).

The apparatus will influence a strip of land 14ft. wide, East and West, and an unlimited distance from South to North.

The grower must not be disappointed if the whole 14ft. of the strip is not electrified the first year. The influence will gradually spread year by year, as more electricity has accumulated in the soil.

The plants assimilating electricity are much more vigorous, and will thereby, later on, when the soil becomes more impregnated, resist the frost and many diseases, which may attack them, much more victoriously.

The Christofleau process is the only process known combining the telluric currents (land magnetism) with the positive electricity or the atmosphere.

The underground wire may be carried for miles and miles in a due North direction from one property to another.

There are many different kinds of Electroculture dealing with industrial electricity, which is imparted into the soil in large quantities, usually of 110 volts for four continuous hours. Then the current is turned off and renewed the next day. Experiments have shown, if this intensity of industrial electricity were imparted into soil for longer than four hours, it would burn and destroy the vegetation.

From an agriculturist's point of view, Mr. Christofleau compares this process to a heavy shower of rain of short duration. After many years of research work in his laboratory, he has succeeded, by means of his apparatus, to capture the positive electricity from the atmosphere, to drain it, and to impart it into the soil in a feeble but continuous manner, which he compares to a slight shower of rain of long duration.

Industrial processes have never been known to show more than 35 per cent. increase in production.

The almost incredible yield obtained by the Christofleau process is due to the feeble current of atmospheric electricity which is imparted into the soil, together with its combination of the terrestrial magnetism.

The wire from the apparatus in the furrow may be carried up hill and down dale, providing the line is still direct North; it can be carried over a creek or river exposed, and the wire again buried on the other side and carried on in the furrow as before.

In the case of a small drain, the wire may be carried through a small earthenware pipe.

As the soil becomes more impregnated with the richness which the apparatus imparts into it, the crops go on increasing during the first, second, third and fourth years; between the fifth and sixth year the soil will have reached its maximum capacity of production, and the crops will remain at their highest, and will not decrease so long as the apparatus is not removed.

The grower is recommended to use manure for the first year, as if the apparatus were not there. It is optional for the grower to use manure or not the second year. After the second year, it is not necessary to use any further manures. The first results will be seen by the foliage, which attains a much darker green, and the leaves will become larger and thicker, due to the larger quantity of nitrogenous products which are imparted into the soil.

The atmospheric electricity runs in stratas or separate layers in the air, each on a different plane, one above the other. The higher the layers from the ground, the greater is the voltage therein. These currents, which are positive currents, are continually passing back wards and forwards in their own particular plane.

The perpendicular pointer and the aerial wires of the apparatus serve as a conductor to pass this positive atmospheric current to the negative current in the ground. It is obvious to see that the higher the post on which the apparatus is placed the more electricity is captured.

Everything grown by electricity is more healthful for human consumption.

With the help of agriculturists, a new era of prosperity is rapidly approaching, and will shortly extend right throughout Australasia, and eventually through the whole world.

It is recommended to paint the post on which the apparatus is placed, to preserve the wood, care being taken that no paint is to be put on the apparatus itself or the wire.

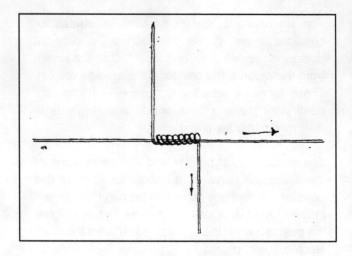

Showing method of fixing dropper wire to main
wires when using an overhead wire on vines.—
page 16.

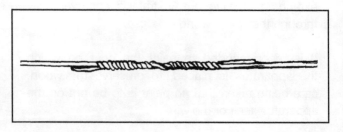

When joining the ends of the wires it is essential
to twist the wires very tightly for about 16 inches;
and to solder the end points.—next page.

POINTS TO REMEMBER

Should you be doubtful on some points please do not hesitate. Your questions will be fully replied to in due course by your local Agent.

The apparatus can be installed at any time, the sooner the better. Electroculture will RAPIDLY SWEETEN AND REJUVENATE land which has been rendered sour by constant cultivation, and will keep the soil well aerated.

It is unwise to wait until the crop is sown before installing the apparatus. The longer it has been erected the more electricity will have been imparted into the soil.

Between the fifth and the sixth years the soil will have reached its maximum capacity of production and will always remain at that. The apparatus must not be removed.

The grower must not be disappointed if the whole of the 14ft. strip is not electrified the first year. The influence will gradually spread year by year as more electricity accumulates in the soil.

When joining the ends of the wires it is essential to splice the wires very tightly for about 16in., and to solder the end points.

The electroculture process of Mr. Christofleau has a really marvellous effect on flowers. The blooms are considerably increased, and are of a remarkable size; the perfume is much more pronounced, and the foliage attains a much richer verdure.

In any commercial undertaking the object is to obtain the maximum of results with the minimum of labour and expense. Please bear in mind that this objective will be attained by using Mr. Christofleau's electroculture process.

When agriculturists become more acquainted with the influence of electricity on culture and vegetation they will realise its manifold and immense advantages.

The results obtained in the first year the apparatus has been installed, will remove this veil of doubt which obscures the minds of the sceptics and the timid. At the end of the second year, when the results will be still more manifest, the agriculturist will realise that electroculture has marked the dawn of a new era in agriculture.

TESTIMONIALS

Experiment Made by Mr. Roger Claret on his Property at Fleury d'Aube (Aube)
(Testimony of the Usher of the Municipality)

In the year 1922 on the 16th of September, I, J. Boyer, Usher of the Civil Tribunal of Narbonne, and there residing, at the request of Mr. Roger Claret, proprietor at Fleury d'Aube, who has certified to me:—That on the 1st April, 1922 he has installed in one of his vineyards at the place called "Les Prés," 28 apparatus of electroculture invented by Mr. Christofleau. That as a result of the influence of those apparatus the crops that are actually on the electrified land are very beautiful, and he requested me to visit his property before the removal of the said crops, to note:—1, the results obtained by the use of those apparatus; 2, to note the difference of the crops with the comparative plots which were of the same soil, the same variety of vines, and which were planted at the same time.

I, J. Boyer, in deference to this request visited the said property and have noted:—1, That on a part of this very large property planted with vines, Mr. Claret has installed 28 apparatus invented by Mr. Christofleau; 2, The vegetation is superb, the shoots are very long, large and abundant, the leaves are very green, large and well developed; 3, The crop on the electrified land is very large; on numerous vines I have counted 35 bunches of large grapes, the berries were very close and very long;

4, This crop is very regular and superior to that of the comparative plots which had been manured. The electrified land had not been manured; 5, Nine hundred and twenty-four vines of the electrified land which were cropped in my presence have produced 100 "comportes"[*1] of grapes and the 2,274 plants would have produced more than 300 comportes; 6, In the other comparative plots of land that were not submitted to the action of the said apparatus, Mr. Claret has declared that 2,000 vines had produced 199 comportes of grapes.

It will be seen that the yield of the land which was submitted to the electro-magnetic treatment was superior to the comparative land. Mr. Claret stated that the comportes had been made up and pressed by the same person and in the same manner.

And of all as above stated I have herewith signed this declaration.

—(Signed) J. BOYER, Usher, Narbonne.

---

1. A "comporte" is a small wooden tub used for carrying the vintage.

Trefoil electrified by the Electroculture process.
Cropped in 1923. Height, 5ft. 3in.

An old Pear Tree laden with fruit.
This tree is so old that before being rejuvenated
by the Electroculture process
it barely carried a few leaves.

Oakdale, via Camden,
4th January, 1927.

Tylors (Australia) Limited,
13 Bridge Street,
Sydney.

Dear Sirs,

I am writing this letter to tell you of the most satisfactory results that I have had from two Christofleau's Electroculture Apparatus. Twelve months ago on a strip of land on which hitherto I had never been able to grow passion fruit successfully and, as I planted passion fruit again, you can see I put the apparatus to a severe test. I planted comparative rows of vines alongside on good land and manured these rows well. The first difference I noticed was the healthy green leaves which appeared on the electrified vines, and also the increased growth, although we had hardly any rain and then only in the winter which is no good to passion vines. Now after 12 months the difference is most marked. The electrified rows of vines are not only healthier with bigger and greener leaves, but the number of fruit is at least double that on the non-electrified rows and the fruit is much bigger.

I am looking forward to even better results from now on, since we have had such good rain. I am sure that these good results are due to the influence of the apparatus. I know that people are sceptical, and I was laughed at here when I first put mine up, but now I have visitors from all parts, and I feel sure that I convince them all before they leave my farm that Electroculture is no joke. I have written to Mr. Christofleau of my success, and I shall shortly be able to order more apparatus from you and I know that Electroculture is doing for my crop all that your pamphlet claims it should.

Wishing you every success.

> Your faithfully,
> —(Sgd.) HARRY LOVELL.

> Steere Street, Collie
> 11/1/27

To Mr. Alex. Trouchet.

Dear Sir,

Having erected one of Mr. Christofleau's Electroculture Apparatus I am pleased to state that I have had very pleasing results. I can safely say that I have gained over three weeks in the ripening of my tomatoes which I planted on ground treated by the Apparatus. The fruit are ripening evenly and are large and of excellent flavour. I have also noted that I had a peach tree and nectarine tree which for three years have been in a deplorable state with curl-leaf, and since installing the Apparatus it bas disappeared entirely. I can put it down to no other agency than Electroculture; I have never sprayed or manured the trees since they were put in. The Apparatus was installed in July, 1926. I have also noted very beneficial results from seedlings of tomatoes and lettuce planted under the influence of the Apparatus. I am quite satisfied from results on comparative plants that are practically on the same class of ground that in two separate crops of tomatoes the result has been identical and those under the influence are far bigger and altogether a superior class of fruit.

I have had a talk to Mr. Bevan, of Allanson, and he is also very pleased with the results of a crop of peas which he put in, and although it was in hungry sand he used super for manure, and he said that he was astonished at the growth and productivity of the crop which was influenced by the wire. A comparative plant with the same manure, on the same class of hungry soil, did not give anything like the crop treated by Electroculture. Mr. Bevan intends to write to you shortly, and you will no doubt be pleased to receive his letter. I visited a Mr. J. Sykes, of Allanson, and he showed me some vines where he had installed one of the Apparatus, and although his vines were put in at the same time, two years, there is wonderful growth on the vines near where the Apparatus wire is buried. With one or two exceptions none of the vines further away from the wire are within feet of them for length of wood.

Wishing you the best of luck.

Yours sincerely,
JOHN McCAUGHAN,

WITNESS:
H. Whiteaker, Justice of Peace,
Collie, W.A.
Jan. 11th, 1927.

La Queue-les-Yvelines,
20th July, 1923.

I, the undersigned, G. Etoc, municipal councillor, produce merchant at La Queue-les-Yvelines, do hereby declare that for the last five years, I have purchased each year the crop of oats grown on a very small field belonging to Mr. J. Christofleau. The production of this small field has increased every year, and this crop which was only of from 120 to 150 bundles has increased this year to 275 bundles, plus 25 bundles which were kept by Mr. Christofleau, yielding therefore a total of 300 bundles. The oats were of splendid quality. The crops were thus doubled since Mr. Christofleau has lived on that property.

—(Signed) G. ETOC.
Witness to Mr. Etoc's signature:
A. JOULAIN.
(Seal of the Municipality).

———————

Montfort L'Amaury,
27th September, 1923.

Mr. Christofleau,
Although the three apparatus I have purchased from you were not installed until the end of March (only six months) I am pleased to inform you the results have been good. I have never had so many

artichokes, some of which were very large. I have had big crops of tomatoes, and the cauliflowers and the salad were very large. My fruit trees seem more vigorous and cause me to hope that next year the results will be even more satisfactory.

—(Signed) A. GROUSSIN,
President of the Horticultural Society of Montfort.

"Riverside," 30 Cook Street,
NEDLANDS, W.A.

To. Mr. Trouchet,
Chemist,
Perth.

Dear Sir,
With reference to Electroculture, of which I see you have the agency. ·
In 1914 when in France with the Expeditionary Force we were halted close to a farm or what appeared to be a farm consisting of house, orchard and large vegetable gardens. As we had eaten nothing but bard tack and Bully Beef for several days, our Major, Lord George Stewart Murray, decided to procure some fruit if possible, and with that intention he took five of us up through the gardens to the house. As we entered the gardens we were astounded to see tomato plants of enormous size heavily laden with fruit. When we met the gentleman of the house he showed us round, and appeared to be remarkably

proud of his produce. He pointed out to us a fig tree that grew in gravel, no earth whatever near the roots. This fact we noticed ourselves. We did not understand the conversation between the Major and Mr. Christofleau, as he afterwards turned out to be, as they were talking in French. We came away eventually with a quantity of beautiful fruit, and this was distributed to the Company. While eating it, practically every man remarked on its beauty, not only in size, but in sweetness and flavour. Later in the day our Major (I regret to say he was killed a few days later) told us that the fruit we had eaten was grown by an invention of the grower. It appeared that he fertilized his ground by electricity derived from the air, and used no manure whatever.

It seems to me that what we saw so many years ago is at last coming into general use.

I am sure that if only prospective users had seen what we saw, they would jump at the system.

I hope you will excuse the liberty I take in writing to you, but I felt that as I have written to the "Sunday Times" and told the Editor of the before mentioned, I would do the same to you.

If you would be so kind I would very much like to see this instrument if you could spare the time to show and explain it to me.

Hoping the above interests you. ·

I am,

Yours faithfully,

—(Sgd.) J. FAIRWEATHER,

Late Sgt. Black Watch.

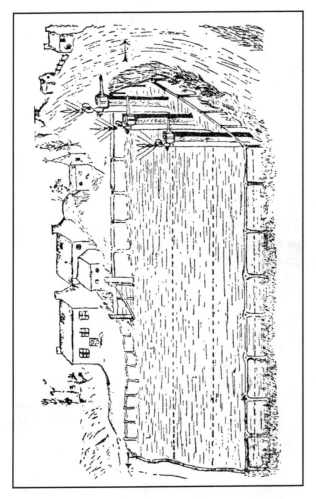

Application to Culture

Note.— Should a neighbour wish to share the cost
of the installation, the wire can easily be extended
into his property.

Box 30, Dowerin, W.A.,
13/6/'27.

Messrs. A. Trouchet & Son,
Forrest Place,
Perth.

Dear Sirs,

Your note to hand re electrified seeds you sent to me after putting through the Electroculture process. I have very much pleasure in telling you that I am very pleased with the results.

The seeds came up well: every one must have germinated. They are now planted out, and are growing well.

Yours truly,
—(Signed) E. E. McHUGH.
Doodlakine, W.A.
16/6/'27.

———————

22 Molloy Street, Bunbury, W.A.,
23rd May, 1927.

Mr. Trouchet,
Padbury's Buildings, PERTH.

Dear Sir,

Your letter to hand a few days ago re our Electroculture process. First of all, I must tell you that Mrs. Illingsworth has gone on a long trip to Europe; she left here last April and I think she will be in England about the middle of June. She does not expect to get back for 12 months.

Well, about those machines we have; I myself think they are wonderful, as we have used no manures at all, and our vegetables have been simply wonderful, also dahlias. The flavour in the peas and beans was simply beautiful, also lettuce. We also had a wonderful lot of rock melons and jam melons.

We are using carrots now that were planted about 9 weeks ago, so one cannot complain about that.

Thanking you,

Yours faithfully,
L. ILLINGSWORTH,
Per Miss Higgie.

Perth, W.A.,
March 25, 1927.

Messrs. A. Trouchet & Son,
Perth.

Re Electroculture.

Dear Sirs,

In reference to experiments carried out by me in my Mt. Barker orchard, I am pleased to say these were highly satisfactory.

I erected the apparatus and carried the wire underground, at a depth of 15 inches, through the orchard, for 10 chains, and then on through two small paddocks, for about 8 chains further, for the purpose of experimenting with crops other than the apples.

I erected the apparatus on November 10th, 1926, and on the 26th of the same month I planted plots of Canadian Wonder Beans and Yorkshire Hero Peas along the wire and check plots 20 feet on one side of the wire, giving them the same quantity of manures, viz., Super 6 parts, Nitrate Soda 1 part, Potash 1 part. Ten weeks after planting, I took samples from the beans, and the result was that the beans on the wire yielded 6 times the weight of the check plot from the same number of plants. The peas also yielded more than double. In both cases, this was due to their coming to maturity so much earlier.

The influence of the Electroculture on the apples was very marked. The Jonathan and Cleopatra being quite two weeks in advance of the trees in the adjacent rows.

Having sold my orchard to Mr. T. Hawley, in February, I had only three months to carry out these experiments, but from what I saw, I am quite convinced that Electroculture will be beneficial to all crops.

The one thing I did want to test was whether the apparatus would cure the Bitter-pit in the Cleopatra apple; but unfortunately I left before they had reached maturity, and did not have a chance of seeing the final result. Still, next year would be the best time to test this, and I hope that Mr. Hawley or Mr. Young will watch this closely for me.

As soon as I am again settled, I shall be pleased to carry out experiments for you where you will have an opportunity of seeing the apparatus thoroughly tested.

I am, yours faithfully,
—(signed) C. J. VAN ZUILECOM.

Iolanthe Street,
Bassendean, W.A.,
9/6/'27.

Messrs. A. Tronchet & Son,
Forrest Place,
Perth.

Dear Sirs,

Re yours of 7th inst. Three sets of tomato seeds were set, two about a fortnight before those treated by you.

The electrified seeds came up much better than the others, and were the only ones to stand the frosts of the last two nights.

I will let you know later on what sort of a crop I get from same, and when I am in a position to do so, I will purchase one of your apparatus.

Yours faithfully,
—(Signed) D. GORDON.

Oats cropped in 1922 in a field without fertilisers
and without irrigation, but influenced by the
Electroculture apparatus.

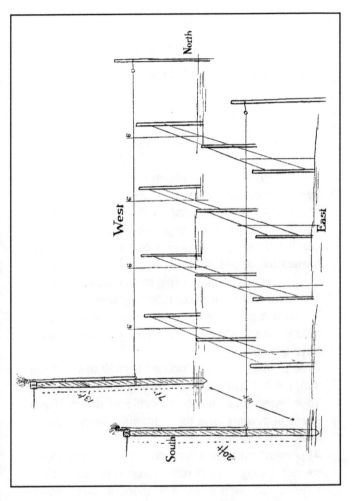

Method of fixing Vines running East and West.
—page 17.

Hack Street,
GOSNELLS,
February 23, 1927.

To Messrs. A. Trouchet & Son,
Perth.

Dear Sirs,

Re Electroculture. It may interest you to know that the Electroculture apparatus installed by my son, appears to be working satisfactorily. The past winter being an exceptionally wet one, growing plants of all description naturally suffered, especially in waterlogged ground. Citrus trees, and other plants coming under the influence of the Electroculture apparatus, appeared to withstand the wet better than those not coming within radius of its influence. Tomato plants, doing exceptionally well.

To get a quicker result, I think the wire should be nearer the surface (not nearly two feet deep), as we have got ours.

Green Jarrah poles are inclined to twist towards the sun, but not sufficiently to make much difference.

Your representative, Mr. Wood, and others, have seen, and were able to compare difference, at a most unfavourable time.

At present we have not much under cultivation, as my son being busy in other directions bas not the time to complete a few alterations to our garden, in order to get the full beneftt of the Electroculture apparatus.

Yours faithfully,

CHAS. H. STAGG.

P.S.—To confirm the above statement, my mandarines sent to market last season realised 14/— per case, against the published prices in the "West Australian," viz., about 11/—.

C.H.S.

Witness this statement,
> February 23rd, 1927.
>> W. F. GUPPY, J.P.,
>> President of the Justices'
>> Association of Western Australia.

———————

Hack Street,
GOSNELLS,
24th February 1927.

To Messrs. A. Trouchet & Son,

Dear Sirs,

In a previous statement I suggested that surface crops would benefit by the apparatus being placed nearer the surface. Our subsequent experience, by growth of Peas, Beans, Lettuce and Tomatoes, have done exceptionally well during the drier period.

Observance justifies the above more particularly without the application of artificial watering.

> Yours faithfully,
>> CHAS. H. STAGG.

Witness this statement, 24th February, 1927.
> W. F. GUPPY, J.P.,
> President of the Justices'
> Association of Western Australia.

"Marbro," New Norcia, W.A.,
13/6/'27.

Messrs. A. Trouchet & Son,
Forrest Place,
Perth.

Dear Sirs,

In reply to yours of 16th inst., the seeds you electrified for me a short time ago have given good results so far.

I had the misfortune of most of the seeds being spoilt, as they were scratched up by the fowls. The seeds which were left seemed to grow wonderfully, as nearly every seed germinated.

Some of the seeds gave poor results last year, but since they were electrified, they germinated and grew rapidly, although the ground was not at its best.

Yours faithfully,
—(Signed) H. HALLIGAN.

Devon Road,
BASSENDEAN, W.A.,
5th January, 1927.

Messrs. A. Trouchet & Son,
Perth.

Dear Sirs,

I purchased an Electroculture apparatus from you last November to try a setting of eggs with. You advised me the machine should be down two or three months to be effective. I found it would be too late to get a broody hen. I had one that persisted in sitting in a place with little or no shade until she became sick.

The apparatus had been erected three weeks, so I gave it a trial; the chickens were due out, according to your booklet, on Sunday night at 10.30 p.m. Monday morning we broke an egg and found a chicken in it; Tuesday afternoon the chicks were out and well. I tried the remaining three and found them infertile. The chicks are strong in spite of the hot weather, and the hen has quite recovered without any special attention. This makes it a day and a half earlier than the usual time, whichwould be Wednesday night or Thursday morning. I consider this very satisfactory, and hope to get the full results in the proper season.

I might state that I have erected this apparatus near a fig tree which has lost its leaves for the last two years when the fruit is ripening, so I am now watching this with interest.

Trusting this will be of interest to you.

Yours faithfully,

—(Signed) THOS. A. WOOD.

Witness this statement,
January 17th, 1927.
W. F. GUPPY, J.P.,
President of the Justices' Association of Western Australia,

Messrs. A. Trouchet & Son,
Perth.

Dear Sirs,

I have much pleasure in replying to your letter of the 7th inst. regarding my electrified seeds. They are doing splendidly. They are better than any flower seeds I have ever yet grown.

As a rule, I have trouble in getting my flower seeds to grow, but these came up in no time, and have grown rapidly ever since.

Yours truly,

—(Signed) Mr. CUOLAHAN.

BRUNSWICK JUNCTION, W.A.,
May 30th, 1927.

Messrs. A. Trouchet & Son,
Perth,

Dear Sirs,·

In my experiments with your Electroculture machine I found that wheat and oats were 75% better than on the plot not treated; and the maize and millet were also improved to the same extent. Other plants were about equal, but it must be taken into consideration that the plots did not receive the work to produce good crops during the hot and dry summer in this country.

Yours faithfully,

—(Signed) O. A. TITLEY.

REPORTS ON RESULTS OBTAINED ON MR. BURGESS'S PROPERTY, BANANA GROWER, GYMPIE ROAD, ASPLEY, QUEENSLAND.

We visited Mr. Burgess on the 4th January. Mr. Burgess has one plant installed, which had been in operation for exactly two (2) months at the date of our visit. Mr. Burgess is remarkably emphatic on the very fine results obtained, even at this date.

He first pointed to a small plot of very poor soil indeed, which had been built up from the refuse from a tannery. This is the first year, for a period of four (4) years since even grass and weeds have grown on this small plot of land. Immediately after the plant was installed, and during extremely dry weather, Mr. Burgess, as an experiment, planted out 18 tomato plants which were badly infested with blight, at the same time planting a few check plants out of the electrified strip. The blight eventually killed these check plants. In the electrified strip, however, the main stem rotted away through the ravages of blight, but fresh roots were sent out from the mother portion of the stem, which are now vigorous and healthy-looking plants. Mr. Burgess states that this result is astounding, and he cannot recall a plant ever recovering after being affected with this disease.

MELONS AND CUCUMBERS.—Mr. Burgess found that melons and cucumbers germinated in the electrified strips between 4 and 5 days. In a check plot some distance away, melon and cucumber seeds took 14 days to germinate. Mr. Burgess states that as far as he can tell, the whole of the seeds in the electrified strip germinated, whereas in the check plot the percentage of germination was poor. He pointed out the very much greater and more vigorous growth in the electrified strips.

BANANAS.— Mr. Burgess is a banana grower of many years experience, and is a very methodic grower. In the electrified strip he has 1st, 2nd and 3rd year plants, and in the case of each plant is able to point to a very marked increase in growth, and he maintains, in all cases, very much healthier plants. Mr. Burgess is already convinced that his 2nd year bananas in the electrified strip will carry a heavy crop, whereas in the soil he is working he is getting no returns from 2nd year plants at present. He remarked particularly on two very sickly plants which, under ordinary circumstances, a grower would pull out and not be bothered with, which in the electrified strip have made really remarkable progress, and within a period of two months picking up from being sickly plants indeed to very fine, healthy and robust plants.

He started off feeling very sceptical of results, but he is now convinced of the results of Electroculture, and he has placed an order for a further 24 plants to be delivered at the rate of 2 per month. He states that when he gets these in, if he can manage it, he will keep on adding until he has electrified the whole of his property.

Price of the Apparatus

THE APPARATUS COSTS £6.
Packed free on Rail Perth.

CASH WITH ORDER—

Exchange to be added on Cheques.

ALEX. TROUCHET & SON

1a Padbury's Buildings, Forest Place,

Perth, Western Australia.

Sole Agents for Australia, New Zealand, Java, Straits Settlements, Federated Malay States, Siam, India, Ceylon, Sumatra, Burma, Demerara, and South Africa.

Electroculture Apparatus Order Form.

Date..................19.........

PLEASE SUPPLY .... Christofleau

Electroculture Apparatus @ £6 each, delivered

f.o.r. or f.o.b. consigned to me at..

I agree to pay rail or motor carriage if incurred and to
forward cheque in payment for the goods (and freight)
within seven days of receipt of same.

Signed ....

....

....

When sending cheque please allow for exchange.

ALEX. TROUCHET & SON

1a Padbury's Buildings, Forest Place,   Perth, Western Australia.

Sole Agents for Australia, New Zealand, Java, Straits Settlements, Federated Malay States, Siam, India, Ceylon,
Sumatra, Burma, Demerara, and South Africa.

DIRECTIONS:

**Do not forget the
correct installation of
the apparatus is the
guarantee of good
results.**

**It is very important
the directions South
and North be correctly
established.**

**Aerials should be AT
LEAST 20 ft.
clear of the ground—
the higher the better,
and the quicker the
results.**

91